Topps

MATCH ATTAX

ANNUAL 2021

WELCOME!

Get ready for loads of football-tastic facts and fun inside this annual. Packed with stats, puzzles and games to play, you'll also find the biggest footballing legends in the world inside.

CLUB GUIDES

From Liverpool FC and Tottenham Hotspur FC to Paris Saint-Germain and Barcelona FC, check out all the top teams in Europe plus their goal-getting players.

PLAY TIME

P 66-67

Play like a pro and turn to page 66 for some tips and tricks to help you become a Match Attax master.

FOOTBALL HEROES

Turn to page 30 for some world-class players, page 40 for some of the highest scorers and page 56 for some historic goals.

AWESOME ACTIVITIES

From word puzzles to spot-the-ball and match-up games, put your skills to the test with all the cool activities inside.

P 46-47

PLAYER MATCH

Turn to page 46 and take the quiz to work out which kind of goal scorer you are. Ready, aim, SHOOT!

P 70-75

DREAM TEAM

Play manger and turn to page 70 to pick your own starting line up from some of the most epic players on the planet.

ANSWERS

You can find all the answers for the puzzles at the back of the book.

MY AWESOME ANNUAL

Here's your chance to show you're a footy expert by picking your favourite players and teams! You can also scribble your sickest skills, reveal your footy dreams and your fave goal ever.

MY NAME: .... AGE: ....

CITY/TOWN: ....

MY SKILLS ....

POSITION: ....

TEAM I PLAY FOR: ....

MY BEST SKILL: ....

MY BEST MOMENT THIS YEAR: ....

....

....

FAVE THREE TEAMS:

1 ....

2 ....

3 ....

....

Look - this is how planes fly. Zoom, zoom!

FAVE UK PLAYER: ....

FAVE WORLDWIDE PLAYER: ....
....

FAVE ALL-TIME PLAYER: ....
....

BEST GOAL SEEN THIS YEAR: ....
....

FOOTY DREAMS FOR THE FUTURE:

I WANT ....

....

....

....

....

ON THE MAP!

Check out the biggest leagues and the greatest clubs from all around Europe!

A geography lesson? Get in!

Double homework for me please, teacher!

LA LIGA SPAIN
TEAMS: 20
STARTED: 1929
One of the most exciting leagues in the world! Barcelona and Real Madrid are the biggest clubs, with Atletico Madrid, Sevilla, Valencia and Villarreal also battling for glory.

PRIMEIRA LIGA PORTUGAL
TEAMS: 18
STARTED: 1934
Watch out for the top trio of Porto, Benfica and Sporting Lisbon scrapping it out for Portugal's Primeira Liga trophy! These three clubs have won every title since 2001, when Boavista were champions.

Bayern Munich won the European Cup three times in a row between **1974** and **1976**

LIGUE 1 FRANCE
TEAMS: 20
STARTED: 1932
In recent years, France's Ligue 1 has been transformed into an epic league to watch. Paris Saint-Germain, Monaco, Marseille and Lyon are the big clubs chasing the title!

EREDIVISIE NETHERLANDS
TEAMS: 18
STARTED: 1956
In their orange kit, the Netherlands national team is well-known around the world. The Eredivisie league is also packed with top talent and teams like Ajax, PSV Eindhoven and Feyenoord.

BUNDESLIGA GERMANY
TEAMS: 18
STARTED: 1963
Bayern Munich, Borussia Dortmund and FC Schalke are just some of Germany's mega clubs. Stars like Robert Lewandowski and Timo Werner bash in great goals every week!

SERIE A ITALY
TEAMS: 20
STARTED: 1898
Famous clubs like Juventus, AC Milan and Inter Milan bring glitz, glamour and goals to Italy's top league! Some of the world's most amazing players have starred in Serie A.

MORE EPIC LEAGUES: Jupiler Pro League **(BELGIUM)** • Premier League **(RUSSIA)** • Primera Division **(ARGENTINA)** • Superleague **(GREECE)** • Bundesliga **(AUSTRIA)** • Super Lig **(TURKEY)** • MLS **(USA & CANADA)** • Brasileirao **(BRAZIL)**

ALL ABOUT

TOTTENHAM HOTSPUR

Here's the lowdown on this top London club's stats and stars, plus the footy facts you need to know!

TACTICS TALK

Manager José Mourinho has turned Tottenham Hotspur into one of the fiercest teams in Europe. With Harry Kane up front, the team usually sets up in a 4-2-3-1 formation. Two holding midfielders play behind forwards Son and Alli, with Aurier and Davies working hard in defence at the back.

STAR TO WATCH

LUCAS MOURA

The winger moved to Tottenham Hotspur after a £25 million switch from PSG. The exciting Brazilian took time to settle at the club, but he's ready to show the fans what a devastating mix of pace and power he has. His right foot can light up Spurs' attacks!

TEAM HERO GLENN HODDLE

One of the most stylish midfielders Spurs have ever produced, Glenn Hoddle starred for the club between 1975 and 1987. He made 377 league appearances, scored 88 goals and won the FA Cup and UEFA Cup. Hoddle also managed England from 1996 to 1999 and Spurs from 2001 to 2003.

3 SICK STARS

HEUNG-MIN SON With his right foot, left foot or head, Son scores all sorts of crucial goals for Tottenham. He links up superbly with Kane.

JAN VERTONGHEN The experienced centre-back keeps Spurs' backline strong and uses his positional sense to cut out danger.

DELE ALLI Using his slick skills, speed, passing and quality shooting, Alli always does the business from his attacking midfield spot.

DID YOU KNOW?

Harry Kane went to the same school as David Beckham – but not at the same time!

★STAR PLAYER

HARRY KANE
POSITION: Striker
BORN: UK, 1993

Goals, goals, goals! That's the best way to describe Harry Kane. The England ace has all the skills – power, vision, accuracy, heading and a natural goal instinct.

ALL ABOUT

MANCHESTER CITY

One of the richest clubs in the world, Manchester City boasts some of the world's top players, who are always seeking to top the footy leagues at home and away.

TACTICS TALK

Manager Pep Guardiola unleashes players like Kevin De Bruyne, Leroy Sane and Raheem Sterling in lightning-quick attacks. Defenders Kyle Walker and Bejamin Mendy race down the wings to cross and set up strikers Sergio Aguero and Gabriel Jesus.

TEAM HERO

GEORGI KINKLADZE

The tricky midfielder was a sensational Manchester City hero between 1995 and 1998. He scored wonder goals and dribbled past defenders as if they were statues. Kinkladze even turned down Barcelona to stay at the club!

STAR TO WATCH

PHIL FODEN

The 18-year-old won the Under-17 World Cup with England in 2017. An exciting midfielder who loves to score and create goals – this left-footed ace always rips it up.

3 SICK STARS

DAVID SILVA The little Spaniard bosses Manchester City's midfield, helping to set up goals.

EDERSON The keeper cost a mega £35 million in 2017, but he was worth every penny.

RAHEEM STERLING Playing on the right, left or in the middle, the England forward can always be counted on.

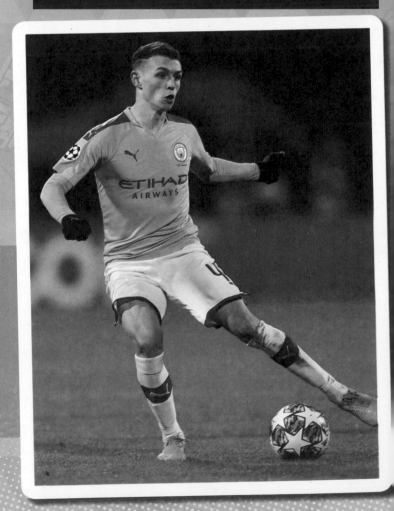

DID YOU KNOW?

This clever midfielder can speak fluent Dutch, French and English.

⭐ STAR PLAYER

KEVIN DE BRUYNE
POSITION: Midfielder
BORN: BELGIUM, 1991

Dazzling De Bruyne is on top form. The brilliant Belgium attacker floats between midfield and attack, whipping laser-guided passes to Aguero and Jesus and delivering perfect free-kicks and corners.

13

WHO SCORED?

Which screamer has beaten the goalie? Follow the lines to find out!

USE YOUR HEAD!

Prove you're champion quality by solving every clue!

Solve each clue in this brain-busting crossword to take home some silverware.

The crossword grid contains the following filled-in answers:

- 6 Down: TACKLE
- 1 Down: VICTORY
- 2 Down: DRIBBLE
- 3 Down: VOLLEY
- 4 Across: CHAMPIONS
- 5 Down: ASSIST
- 7 Across: GOALKEEPER
- 8 Down: REFEREE
- 9 Across: PENALTY

DOWN

1 Another word for a win. (7)

2 To move the ball up the pitch close to your body. (7)

3 To strike the ball before it touches the ground. (6)

5 The last pass before a goal is scored. (6)

6 When you steal the ball from an opponent. (6)

8 The person in charge of a football match. (7)

ACROSS

4 The team that wins the league will be the _ _ _ _ _ _ _ _ _. (9)

7 The only person that can handle the ball on the pitch. (10)

9 This is awarded if a foul is committed in the 18-yard box. (7)

ALL ABOUT

LIVERPOOL FC

Jurgen Klopp's entertaining and talented team always plays to the crowd to produce exciting games and thrilling results.

TACTICS TALK

With an epic attacking trio of Mohamed Salah, Roberto Firmino and Sadio Mane, manager Klopp usually starts with a 4-3-3 set up, with Virgil Van Dijk controlling the defence and captain Jordan Henderson bossing central midfield.

3 SICK STARS

ROBERTO FIRMINO The slick-skilled Brazilian has become a top-class No.9 for The Reds with his pace and penalty box skills.

ALEX OXLADE-CHAMBERLAIN Liverpool paid £35 million for the versatile midfielder. He's worth every penny with his non-stop running and goal threat.

JORDAN HENDERSON He skippers the team very well, making vital tackles and precise passes to release Liverpool's lightning-quick attackers.

STAR TO WATCH

TRENT ALEXANDER-ARNOLD

The young defender was born in Liverpool and is a first-team regular for The Reds, the team he supported as a boy. Alexander-Arnold also plays for England and is one of the best full-backs in the world on his current form.

Sssh! I'm awesome, but let's keep it a secret.

TEAM HERO STEVEN GERRARD

UEFA Champions League, FA Cup, League Cup, UEFA Super Cup – former Liverpool FC captain Steven Gerrard has bags of silverware! Between 1998 and 2015, the central midfielder scored 120 league goals and 41 in Europe. Stevie G mixed power, vision and quality passing to awesome effect.

DID YOU KNOW?

Virgil Van Dijk joined The Reds for **£75** million in 2018, which was a world record for a defender.

★STAR PLAYER

MOHAMED SALAH
POSITION: Forward
BORN: Egypt, 1992

Wow! What skills Mohamed Salah brings to Liverpool FC! After joining in summer 2017, the skillful Egyptian's left-foot defeated defenders and combined with slick skills and turbo speed, it's no surprise that Salah is one the most feared goal scorers.

17

GAME ON!

1

Cut out the template to make a kickin' doorhanger for your bedroom door.

2

Choose which side you want to hang it on depending on your Match Attax game time.

75

60

KEEP OUT!
GAME IN PROGRESS!

GAME ON!
COME ON IN!

GOAL GETTERS!

We're never all going to fit in there!

Fit these footballing greats into the grid below.

- HIGUAIN
- ALISSON
- ISCO
- RONALDO
- FIRMINO
- STERLING
- NEYMAR
- DZEKO
- KANE
- LOVREN
- BALE
- ROBBEN
- LEWANDOWSKI
- MESSI

HIGUAIN

ALISSON (vertical) ISCO

LEWANDOWSKI

FIRMINO

RONALDO

ROBBEN BEN

DZEKO

NEYMAR

KANE

MESSI

LOVREN

BALE

STERLING

ANSWERS AT BACK OF BOOK.

21

ALL ABOUT

CHELSEA

This top London team have a trophy cabinet full of silverware and a squad that's packed with world-class heroes.

TACTICS TALK

Fank Lampard, Chelsea's manager approaches the games with an attacking mentality. His preference for a passing style makes for exciting games and he works to utilise the skills of three of his most valuable players, Kante, Abraham and Mount.

3 SICK STARS

KEPA ARRIZABALAGA Controls his goal with incredible saves and reflexes, making him a vital part of the team.

TAMMY ABRAHAM This young striker is a beast in the box and a clinical goal scorer.

WILLIAN The busy Brazilian is always full of energy, skill and pace. He strikes a sweet free-kick with his right boot, too!

TEAM HERO

FRANK LAMPARD

Goal scoring midfielder Lampard played for The Blues from 2001 to 2014. In that time he clocked up 648 games, bagged a record 211 goals and secured 11 major honours. Lamps is also the highest-scoring midfielder in UK history with 177 goals.

STAR TO WATCH

ROSS BARKLEY

Injury meant the England midfielder hardly played for Chelsea at first, after joining from Everton. When he's fully fit, the £15 million man loves to boss the pitch and break forward to support attacks. Big things are expected of this exciting player!

★ STAR PLAYER

MARCOS ALONSO
POSITION: Defender
BORN: SPAIN, 1990

Alonso was born in Madrid and is the son
and grandson of former Spain internationals.
Currently he has made the starting line up for
5 games in the 2019/20 UEFA Champions League
with an 80% tackle success rate.

DID YOU KNOW?

Olivier Giroud is an awesome header of the ball - with many of his most memorable goals scored with his head.

23

MATCH REPORT

Puzzle over these questions from a crazy cup tie (we made up the result). How well will you score?

1 If kick-off is at 3pm and the first half lasts 45 minutes, draw the hands on the clock to show when half-time is.

2 Sterling scores a goal at 3:19. How many minutes is this into the game?

ANSWER:

3 Firmino equalises 4 minutes before half-time. In which minute did he score?

ANSWER:

4 Half-time lasts 15 minutes. When will it be time to kick off again?

ANSWER:

5 Stones receives a yellow card 11 minutes after half-time. How many minutes have been played altogether?

ANSWER:

6 Salah gets injured 2 minutes later. How many minutes have been played now?

ANSWER:

7 Mane comes on as a sub after 76 minutes. How many minutes will he play for if the game is won in 90 minutes?

ANSWER:

8 Lallana is shown a red card with just two minutes left on the clock. In which minute was he sent off?

ANSWER:

9 The match goes to extra-time, with 30 minutes added on. How many minutes will have been played altogether?

ANSWER:

10 It's a penalty shootout! Manchester City win 4–2 on penalties. How many penalties found the back of the net?

ANSWER:

GO FOR GOAL!

START

Help this attacking player dribble through the maze, dodging defenders along the way to reach the goal.

GOAL

ANSWERS AT BACK OF BOOK.

LOOKIN' FOR LEGENDS!

**These footballing stars are red hot!
Can you find them all in the grid?**

```
H I Q O S D M V O L J Z L B M R
I T C B Z T A T U D O Z J H E I
D I F L E N R L B N L Q Y D O L
N T H A G G T Y Z A I A D T C B
E M R K W R I I A K C E N A S O
M U Z W W A N O R D Y C B O I N
A O G U E D E S A N I U A L R A
R X A S Y B Z E E R S C Q S M T
R S Q M R L V B T Q J S D U B I
A R B X A J C M U S T S I Q R I
L U P U G B P E S A P S A U X I
L M T A K K T S B N U G Q Y L N
I O H J U S I S H Z D Z H A H A
A M D U X L P I E Y E P I N H Z
F G O F R J I R T F N Z O N Z I
G R I E Z M A N N H S Y C S N I
U L H K T U G A H O I S N E S A
C A S D S L F K I O F B W H O R
```

- ◯ BONATINI
- ◯ BEN YEDDER
- ◯ ASENSIO
- ◯ UMTITI
- ◯ BACCA
- ◯ MESSI
- ◯ LUIS
- ◯ SUAREZ
- ◯ OBLAK
- ◯ PAULINHO
- ◯ ILLARRAMENDI
- ◯ MARTINEZ
- ◯ ASPAS
- ◯ BUSQUETS
- ◯ ISCO
- ◯ GUEDES
- ◯ RONALDO
- ◯ GRIEZMANN

Can you pick out the letters with a yellow spot behind them and rearrange them to spell out a football-related word.

ALL ABOUT

BARCELONA

Superstar Spanish club Barcelona is packed with talent, trophies and top new signings every year! Discover more about Barca's amazing story and success...

BRILL BARCA!

You could fill a book with the victories, epic players and fantastic history of Barcelona! This skilful Spanish team have been the most eye-catching club this century and had some of the best players on the planet. Footy legends like Andres Iniesta, Gerard Pique and Lionel Messi came through the club's famous youth system and heroes such as Luis Suarez and Ousmane Dembele arrived in mega transfers.

STARS TO WATCH...

LUIS SUAREZ	**OUSMANE DEMBELE**	**GERARD PIQUE**
STRIKER	WINGER	DEFENDER
Powerful shots & top tricks	Dribble & speed king	Strong & clever on the ball

Smile for the camera!

Messi started to play for **Barcelona's academy** when he was just 13 years old.

MAGIC MESSI

Since scoring his first goal for Barcelona in 2005 aged 17, he's the club's all-time top scorer and has won over 30 trophies in Spain. Messi is probably the most exciting player ever – he can dribble, trick or speed past defenders and creates goals and chances from nothing. The Argentine ace really is a little wizard with a magical left foot!

TROPHY TALK

It's a good job the Camp Nou stadium is so huge, because Barca need a massive place to show off all their trophies! Up to 2017, the club had picked up 24 La Liga titles, five UEFA Champions League, three FIFA Club World Cups, 29 Copa del Rey and 12 more top Euro honours. If there was a prize for Coolest World Club, they'd walk off with that one too!

CAPTAIN: Lionel Messi **NEW SIGNING:** Matheus Fernandes **ATTACKING MIDFIELDER:** Alex Collado

WORLD

★ ★ ★ ★ ★

SUPERSTARS

From Pele to Cruyff and Maradona to Maldini, discover why this bunch of brilliant world superstars are the biggest heroes, past and present.

Help! This thing is well heavy!

DIEGO MARADONA

MAIN CLUBS: Boca Juniors, Napoli, Barcelona

POSITION: STRIKER

COUNTRY: Argentina

- Lead Napoli to Serie A title in 1987 and 1990
- Superstar of the 1986 World Cup
- Strength, skills and epic dribbling

EUSEBIO

MAIN CLUB: Benfica

POSITION: Striker

COUNTRY: Portugal

- Incredible record of 727 goals in 715 Benfica games
- Golden Boot winner at 1966 World Cup
- Deadly hitman with 11 titles in Portugal

RONALDINHO

MAIN CLUBS: AC Milan, Barcelona, PSG

POSITION: Forward

COUNTRY: Brazil

- Super skilful winger or striker
- La Liga, Serie A and UEFA Champions League winner
- World Cup hero with Brazil in 2002

ALFREDO DI STEFANO

MAIN CLUB: Real Madrid
POSITION: Striker
COUNTRY: Spain and Argentina

- Five European Cup victories
- Superstar striker in 1950s and '60s
- Powerful, with laser-like shooting

PELE

MAIN CLUB: Santos
POSITION: Striker
COUNTRY: Brazil

- Won World Cup in 1958, 1962 and 1970
- Deadly accurate in front of goal
- Career record of 1,281 goals

GEORGE BEST

MAIN CLUB: Manchester United
POSITION: Forward
COUNTRY: Northern Ireland

- Red Devils megastar in 1960s and '70s
- Deadly dribbling, speed, tricks and shooting
- 179 goals in 470 Manchester United games

PAOLO MALDINI

CLUB: AC Milan
POSITION: Defender
COUNTRY: Italy

- Played 902 games and won 26 trophies with Milan
- Cool on the ball, tough, with a sweet left foot
- Five times UEFA Champions League winner

I've got more medals than you've had hot dinners!

31

WORLD ★★★★★
SUPERSTARS

FRANZ BECKENBAUER

MAIN CLUB: Bayern Munich
POSITION: Defender
COUNTRY: Germany

- Stylish centre-back and sweeper
- Three European Cups and five Bundesligas
- World Cup winner as player and coach

RONALDO

MAIN CLUBS: Real Madrid, Inter Milan and Barcelona
POSITION: Striker
COUNTRY: Brazil

- World Cup star in 1998, 2002, 2006
- Amazing speed, tricks and shooting
- Two La Liga titles with Real Madrid

MICHEL PLATINI

MAIN CLUBS: Juventus, St-Etienne
POSITION: Forward
COUNTRY: France

- Serie A and European Cup winner
- Amazing goalscorer and leader
- Speed, skills and intelligence

GERD MULLER

MAIN CLUB: Bayern Munich
POSITION: Striker
COUNTRY: Germany

- Club record 533 goals for Bayern
- Five Bundesliga and three European Cup titles
- World Cup winner in 1974

MIROSLAV KLOSE

MAIN CLUBS: Lazio, Bayern Munich, Werder Bremen
POSITION: Striker
COUNTRY: Germany

- Germany legend with 16 World Cup finals goals
- Record 71 strikes in 137 international games
- Awesome header of the ball

ROBERTO BAGGIO

MAIN CLUBS: AC Milan, Juventus, Fiorentina
POSITION: Forward
COUNTRY: Italy

- Serie A winner with Juventus and Milan
- Amazing dribbling and free-kicks
- Starred at 1990, 1994 and 1998 World Cup

JOHAN CRUYFF

MAIN CLUBS: Ajax, Barcelona
POSITION: Forward
COUNTRY: Netherlands

- Stylish, skilful and great vision
- Three European Player of the Year awards
- European Cup winner as player and coach

You can call me Zizou!

Zidane starred for France at the 2006, 2002 and 1998 World Cup.

ZINEDINE ZIDANE

MAIN CLUBS: Real Madrid, Juventus
POSITION: Midfielder
COUNTRY: France

- Three World Player of the Year trophies
- World Cup and Champions League winner
- Magical skills, control, power and passing

33

ALL ABOUT

BAYERN MUNICH

German clubs don't come any bigger than the brilliant Bayern Munich!
The Bundesliga greats are a worldwide superpower with stacks of success.

PLAYER POWER

With the likes of Thomas Muller, Joshua Kimmich and Thiago Alcantara Bayern's squad is one of the best in Europe. Plus, Bayern have the goalscoring skills of Robert Lewandowski – one of the most dangerous strikers on the planet!

GERMAN GIANTS

Thanks to a record 28 German titles between 1932 and 2019, Bayern Munich's trophy cabinet is absolutely stuffed! The last time they finished outside of the top two was way back in 2007 and they now have seven league championships in a row. With over 30 German cups and five UEFA Champions Leagues up to 2013, it's a huge shock if Bayern don't win at least one trophy every season.

STARS TO WATCH...

★★★☆☆

THOMAS MULLER
FORWARD
Goalscorer & creator

KINGSLEY COMAN
WINGER
Speedy & skilful

MANUEL NEUER
GOALKEEPER
Awesome saves & kicking

Robert Lewandowski first wore the Bayern No.9 in **2014** after moving from Bundesliga rivals Borussia Dortmund.

In 2015, Bayern's No.9 scored a record **five** Bundesliga goals in just **nine** minutes against Wolfsburg.

Lewandowski's a goal creator too, clocking up **94** assists in **397** appearances for club and country.

Robert needed just **136** games to crack in his **100th** Bayern Munich goal in all competitions.

He helped Poland reach the **2018** World Cup by netting a European record of **16** goals in qualifying.

Lewandowski moved into the top ten all-time UEFA Champions League goal scorers in 2018 with his **45th** strike in **67** games.

The Poland captain has been voted his country's Player of the Year **seven** times in a row!

In **250** Bundesliga games, Robert smashed an unbelievable **171** goals!

In **2013** he blasted **four** goals in a UEFA Champions League semi-final for Borussia Dortmund against Real Madrid.

CAPTAIN: Manuel Neuer **TOP SCORER:** Gerd Muller (533) **YOUNG STAR:** Christian Fruchtl

GAME TIME!

Find a friend and challenge them to this fun game.

1 Take it in turns to draw a vertical or horizontal line between each dot on the board below.

2 Each time you complete a box, mark your initials inside it.

36

3 An empty box is worth 1 point, a football box is worth 2 points, a striker box is worth 3 points and a red card box is worth -1 point.

4 When all the dots have been joined up, add up your scores. The player with the most points, wins. Don't worry if you lose, just play again on the board below.

SPOT THE STRIKERS

```
                                                    S   F   Q
                                            A   S   E   S   C   M
                                            D   E   S   C   O   B
                                        Q   M   O   O   S   Y
                                    Z   U   C   A   L   T   D
                            S   I   N   C   L   I   R   E   A   C
                    S   O   T   M   S   H   A   O   C   R   V   L
            C   E   J   K   W   J   W   S   M   E   O   H   R
            N   L   U   Y   A   W   N   E   A   M   K   F
        A   A   K   E   Q   Y   L   A   P   S   F   J   U   Q
        I   K   L   Q   Z   D   H   R   I   S   H   L   E   S
        S   S   E   C   B   D   C   H   J   K   Z   R   R   N
        W   D   C   G   O   X   H   J   C   Q   M   R   Y   M
        Q   R   G   N   H   C   C   Q   Q   N   F   T   D   G   Q
        F   O   N   F   C   M   Q   O   L   N   A   A   Y   Q   E
        U   I   F   Z   M   O   R   A   T   B   U   U   A   Z
            G   N   N   A   Y   E   E   M   A   B           R
```

Can you find these goal kings hiding in the boot?

KANE	MESSI	SINCLAIR
HIGUAIN	FIRMINO	VARDY
RONALDO	COSTA	GRIEZMANN
NEYMAR	MORATA	AGUERO
MORELOS	SANCHEZ	AUBAMEYANG
BENZEMA	CAVANI	

```
X G Q N G W O V D A W
D H I G U A I N S A C Y
C G Q N G M O S N A R Y N
T P M C R M S V N C H E Z
D L Q I E C U I B L S T N
N R B S I S B R X J J D O
R G A X Z A O N I M R I F
L B O V M C P S O Q B H A
Q K B E A A L L N R I S X
A F Y H N V O R E U G A X
T A G E N A P R Y R P R K
N A M E Z N E B M D G U Q
O A H Y M I F C A U I W Y
U R J Q Z V C R R Y P A T
M B A P Y J F V P Q V E D
S X X T Y Y B B C F O B
```

BATTLE OF THE BIG GUNS!

Ronaldo, Messi and Neymar have been voted the three best players on the planet. Check out their goals, stats and trophy hauls!

CRISTIANO RONALDO

Club: Juventus

Position: Left Winger

Full name: Cristiano Ronaldo dos Santos Aveiro

Nickname: Ronnie, CR7

Date of Birth: 5 February, 1985

Place of Birth: Funchal, Madeira, Portugal

Height: 1.87 m **Weight:** 84 kg

Left or Right Footed: Both

International Team: Portugal

Game appearances:	836
Goals:	626
Assists:	219
Yellow cards:	99
Red cards:	7
UEFA Champions League Winner :	7

This is my totally serious about scoring face.

Ronaldo is head and shoulders above the rest of the world when it comes to UEFA Champions League goals – by April 2018, he'd scored **117** times in the competition!

40

NEYMAR JR

Club: Paris Saint-Germain

Position: Forward

Full name: Neymar da Silva Santos Júnior

Nicknames: 'O Joia' (The gem), NJR

Date of Birth: 5 February, 1992

Place of Birth: São Paulo, Brazil

Height: 1.75 m **Weight:** 68 kg

Left or Right Footed: Both

International Team: Brazil

Game appearances:	400
Goals:	244
Assists:	151
Yellow cards:	105
Red cards:	2
UEFA Champions League Winner :	1

During his time at Barcelona, **Messi** has won **30** major honours. Let's hope his trophy cabinet is big enough!

LIONEL MESSI

Club: Barcelona

Position: Forward

Full name: Lionel Andrés Messi Cuccittini

Nicknames: 'La Pulga' (The Flea)

Date of Birth: 24 June, 1987

Place of Birth: Rosario, Argentina

Height: 1.70 m **Weight:** 72 kg

Left or Right Footed: Left

International Team: Argentina

Neymar's massive **£198-million** move from Barcelona to Paris Saint-Germain smashed the world-record fee for a transfer.

Game appearances:	718
Goals:	627
Assists:	261
Yellow cards:	75
Red cards:	0
UEFA Champions League Winner :	4

PUZZLE IT OUT

Can you work out the sums below using the answers already given?

 + + = 18

 + + = 9

 x − = 12

 1 + + =

 2 x + − =

 3 x + =

 4 − + =

SPOT THE BALL

Can you count up all the large, medium and small balls in the puzzle below?

I counted _____ large balls.

I counted _____ medium balls.

I counted _____ small balls.

ANSWERS AT BACK OF BOOK.

43

ALL ABOUT

JUVENTUS

Juventus boss Serie A! The Italian masters have fantastic players, bags of trophies and amazing fans. Take a close look at the awesome Italians...

PLAYER POWER

Juventus' squad is boosted by many of Serie A's top stars. After selling Paul Pogba to Manchester United in 2016, they bought striker Gonzalo Higuain for a huge £75 million. Higuan scored 24 league goals in his first season and he's supported in attack by Paulo Dybala and Cristiano Ronaldo. Gianluigi Buffon has been a legendary keeper since joining in 2001 and Andrea Barzagli and Giorgio Chiellini proved a tough centre-back duo.

TROPHY TALK

In 2019, Juventus picked up a record 35th Italian top-flight championship. It was also the first time any club had won eight Serie A titles in a row! The Old Lady are European heavyweights with two UEFA Champions League crowns, but they have lost Europe's biggest final seven times, including 2017 and 2015. Up to 2019, Juve also had 13 wins Coppa Italia and eight Italian Super Cup trophies. There's plenty of silverware on show!

STARS TO WATCH...

MIRALEM PJANIC
MIDFIELDER
Cool head bosses games

JUAN CUADRADO
WINGER
Speed & slick right foot

SAMI KHEDIRA
MIDFIELDER
Brings goals & epic passing

GONZALO HIGUAIN
STRIKER
Pure goal machine

Forward **Paulo Dybala** first wore No.10 for Juventus in August 2017. He had No.21 when he joined from Palermo in 2015.

Before Juventus, the attacker spent three seasons in Serie A with **Palermo**.

He scored **45** Serie A goals in his first **86** games for Juve.

Dybala also plays for Argentina and made his first international appearance in **2015**.

The Juventus No.10 is a speedy forward and can reach speeds of **29 km** per hour on the pitch!

His first UEFA Champions League goal was against Bayern Munich in **2016**.

He was born in November **1993**.

In **2017–18**, Dybala scored **12** of his first **15** Serie A goals with his **left** foot.

He's a **free-kick** king who loves to whip the ball over the wall!

His favourite foot is his **left**.

CAPTAIN: Giorgio Chiellini   **BIG BUY:** Gonzalo Higuain (£75M in 2016)   **YOUNG STAR:** Rodrigo Bentancur

WHICH GOALSCORER ARE YOU?

START

Does your game use **speed and vision**, or are you a **powerful player** who battles defenders?

SPEED

POWER

Do you usually take **penalties** for your team?

NO

YES

Can you score with **both** your right and left feet?

YES

Do you often try to score from **free-kicks**?

YES

NO

Are you famous for a **leaping goal celebration**?

NO

YES

Would you prefer to play in a **red** kit or a **blue** kit?

RED

BLUE

NO

NO

Have you scored lots of **headed goals** in your league?

YES

YOU'RE

MO SALAH

The Liverpool FC goal machine is super speedy, lets rip with his lethal left foot and looks awesome in red!

YOU'RE

EDEN HAZARD

Hazard mixes his pace and skills on the pitch and can score spectacular goals from penalties, free-kicks and outside the box!

YOU'RE

CRISTIANO RONALDO

The Juventus striker has netted over 100 headers and constantly causes headaches for defenders.

47

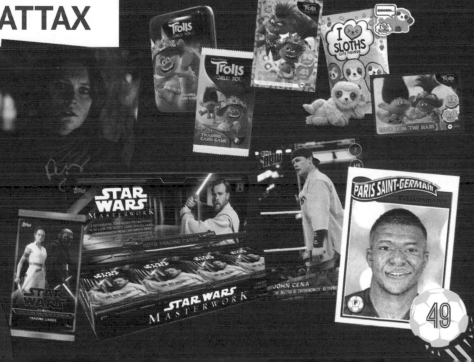

ALL ABOUT

REAL MADRID

Goals, superstars, trophies and top transfers – Real Madrid fans always have plenty to cheer about at the Bernabeu!

GAME PLAN

Zinedine Zidane has packed his team with goalscoring talent. Gareth Bale and Karim Benzema have over 250 club strikes between them and midfielders Marco Asensio, Isco, Luka Modric and Toni Kroos set up stacks of chances. Rock-hard defender Sergio Ramos also loves to hit the net!

TROPHY TALK

UEFA Champions League, La Liga, FIFA Club World Cup, UEFA Super Cup trophies... Real Madrid have lifted them all this decade! The Whites won 33 league titles between 1932 and 2017 and became the first club to win consecutive UEFA Champions League titles in 2016 and 2017. That year they won Europe's top prize for a record 12th time.

STARS TO WATCH...

JAMES RODRÍGUEZ
MIDFIELDER
Creative passer

RAPHAEL VARANE
DEFENDER
Perfect tackler

ISCO
MIDFIELDER
Trickster with ace shooting

GARETH BALE
FORWARD
Skilful left foot

Marcelo Da Silva was born in **1988** in Rio de Janeiro, **Brazil**.

He weighs 75kg and is **1.74m** tall.

Marcelo **De Silva** has won 4 FIFA Club World Cups, 3 European Super Cups, 4 National Leagues, 2 Spanish Cups, 4 Spanish Super Cups and 1 Olympic Silver Medal.

CAPTAIN: Sergio Ramos **BIG BUY:** Gareth Bale (£85m in 2013) **YOUNG STAR:** Éder Militao

BALL BOGGLE

How many words can you spot in the word grid below? Letters must join in the proper sequence of the word and can be found by looking upwards, downwards, sideways and diagonally.

```
G  O  A  M
C  T  L  B
H  I  R  L
P  D  A  W
```

BALL

....

....

....

....

SOCCER SUDOKU

1

Doodle these icons into the grids below to complete the puzzles. There can only be one of each icon in every row and column.

2

ANSWERS AT BACK OF BOOK.

53

ALL ABOUT

ATLETICO MADRID

Barcelona and Real Madrid need to watch out – Atletico Madrid are shooting for Spanish glory! It's time to reveal just how talented the team is…

SLICK STADIUM

Atletico moved into their amazing new stadium, the Wanda Metropolitano, at the start of the 2017–18 season. Before that they played at the Estadio Vicente Calderon for over 50 years. Their new ground holds approximately 68,000 fans, allows spectators to be closer to the pitch and has over 800 large TV screens.

TROPHY TALK

Awesome Atletico Madrid are the third most successful club in La Liga, after Real Madrid and Barcelona. Between 1940 and 2014 they lifted ten championships and secured ten Copa del Rey wins. Legendary manager Diego Simeone is the man behind their recent success, but they lost the 2014 and 2016 UEFA Champions League finals to fierce city rivals Real Madrid.

STARS TO WATCH…

RENAN LODI
DEFENDER
Amazing heading skills

KOKE
MIDFIELDER
Bosses games with ease

SAUL NIGUEZ
MIDFIELDER
Creative & energetic

GOAL GETTERS

Although Diego Simeone has turned Atletico Madrid into a very tough team to beat with powerful defenders, they also have some of the best attacking talent in Spain! Diego Costa fires in the goals in the league and Europe. Sergio Aguero, Radamel Falcao and Diego Forlan have all smashed the net for Atletico in the 21st century!

CAPTAINS: Koke is the official captain with Oblak as vice-captain and Gimenez as third captain.

GOLDEN GREATS

Check out these stats and facts about the golden goalscorers who have picked up Europe's hottest striking prize – the Golden Shoe!

The **Golden Shoe** is given to the highest-scoring player in European league footy each season.

Goals scored in the big five leagues (England, Germany, France, Italy and Spain) earn two points. Each goal in smaller leagues is worth 1 or 1.5 points.

It began in 1968, with Benfica striker **Eusebio** taking the trophy with **42** league goals.

Portuguese master!

Thierry Henry has also racked up two Golden Shoe awards, winning in **2004** and **2005**.

Lionel Messi was presented with his sixth European Golden Shoe award in 2019 after netting 36 goals in Barcelona's triumphant La Liga campaign in 2018/19.

Luis Suarez scooped the European Golden Shoe in 2014 (tied with Ronaldo) and in 2016.

I'll add this to my collection!

Cristiano Ronaldo has also racked up four Golden Shoe awards, winning in **2008**, **2011**, **2014** and **2015**.

ALL ABOUT

VALENCIA FC

On the sunny east coast of Spain, Valencia FC's bright talents hope to take the club back to their European glory days!

GAME PLAN

Valencia FC is the third most supported team behind Barcelona and Real Madrid. After achieving much success with manager Marcelino, including a return to the UEFA Champions League and winning the Copa del Rey for the first time since 2008, the club is now managed by Albert Celades López, who is a former Spanish former defensive midfielder.

TROPHY TALK

You have to go back to 2008 for Valencia FC's last major honour, when Juan Mata and David Villa helped them to the Copa del Rey. But, at the start of this century, Valencia FC were one of the top teams in Europe. Under manager Rafael Benitez they were La Liga champs in 2002 and 2004 and took the UEFA Cup and UEFA European Super Cup around that time, too.

STARS TO WATCH...

FRANCIS COQUELIN
MIDFIELDER
Plays anywhere in midfield

GABRIEL PAULISTA
DEFENDER
Top tackling

JUAME DOMÉNECH
GOALKEEPER
Strong in the box

PLAYER POWER

The backbone of Valencia FC is Ezequiel Garay in defence, Dani Parejo and Geoffrey Kondogbia controlling midfield and Rodrigo snapping in attack. Francis Coquelin was signed from Arsenal to boost the middle of the pitch, with Goncalo Guedes and Carlos Soler defending and running down the wings. Valencia FC created a top team work-rate to take on the bigger Spanish teams!

CAPTAIN: Dani Parejo **TOP SCORER:** Maxi Gómez **YOUNG STAR:** Ferran Torres

PASS THE BALL

Can you help player 1 dribble the ball through the maze to the centre of the pitch then back to player 2?

PLAYER 1

PLAYER 2

CENTRE

TRAINING TROUBLE

Oops! These players are late for training. Which route will get them to the training ground?

START

A B C D

FINISH

ALL ABOUT

BORUSSIA DORTMUND

With Bundesliga and UEFA Champions League trophies, Borussia Dortmund can flex their muscles with the best clubs in Europe! Check out their top stats and stars.

GROUND FORCE

The atmosphere at the mighty Signal Iduna Park is unlike anywhere else in Germany! It's the biggest ground in the country, with its south stand alone housing 24,454 fans, and generates a monster sound when Dortmund turn on the style and hit the net. The stadium opened in 1974 and every Bundesliga player looks forward to running out at this legendary venue.

TROPHY TALK

Borussia Dortmund are a powerful European club, with impressive trophy counts at home and abroad. They've won three Bundesliga titles in the 21st century, with eight in total, plus nine major German cups up to 2017. In 1997, Dortmund were the first German club to win the UEFA Champions League and were runners-up to Bayern Munich in 2013.

STARS TO WATCH...

| **JULIAN BRANDT** MIDFIELDER Clever goalscorer | **MARCO REUS** STRIKER Ace attacking skills | **ROMAN BURKI** GOALKEEPER Last man standing |

EPIC ENGLAND STAR

Tricky teenager Jadon Sancho surprisingly left Manchester City in 2017 to make his mark in the Bundesliga. The midfielder helped England win the Under-17 World Cup and with Dortmund's No.7 shirt, Sancho's expected to become a key player for the German giants. He's full of slick skills and loves to burst forward to create and score goals!

CAPTAIN: Marco Reus **TOP SCORER:** Jadon Sancho **MIDFIELD ANCHOR:** Axel Witsel

ALL ABOUT

RB LEIPZIG

An exciting team with an amazing success story in recent years – RB Leipzig are Bundesliga giants with a big future!

UEFA CHAMPIONS LEAGUE

Just eight years after their very first game, RB Leipzig played in the UEFA Champions League! In the 2017-18 season the club won twice and drew one game in Group G, with top deliverer Emil Forsberg scoring their first European goal. In the UEFA Europa League that season, The Bulls pulled off another shock by beating Serie A leaders Napoli. The Germans will definitely be a Euro force for years to come.

FAST FORWARD

RB Leipzig only formed in 2009 – you might have smelly footy socks nearly as old as that! They started out in the fifth division of German footy and by 2016 they'd stormed to the Bundesliga after four exciting promotions. The Bulls' first season in the top division was amazing – they won 20 games, collected 67 points and finished runners-up to Bayern Munich. It's never boring being a RB Leipzig fan!

STARS TO WATCH...

DAYOT UPAMECANO
DEFENDER
Talented on the ball

TIMO WERNER
STRIKER
Star German goalscorer

YUSSUF POULSEN
STRIKER
Strong team player

PETER GULACSI
GOALKEEPER
Awesome shot-stopper

RB LEIPZIG TIMELINE

2010 Oberliga champions
2011 Regionalliga fourth
2012 Regionalliga third
2013 Regionalliga champions
2014 3. Liga runners-up
2015 2. Bundesliga fifth
2016 2. Bundesliga runners-up
2017 Bundesliga runners-up
2018 Bundesliga sixth
2019 Bundesliga third

NABY KEITA

Behind RB Leipzig's sensational Bundesliga rise was power-packed central midfielder, Naby Keita. The Guinea star joined the team in 2016 and hit 15 goals and ten assists in his first 57 games. He was like Lionel Messi and N'Golo Kante all rolled into one – a skilful attacking star who won the ball in the middle of the pitch for The Bulls. Sadly for the team he was bought by Liverpool FC in 2018 and is now delighting the fans in Anfield with his onfield skills.

CAPTAIN: Willi Orban **SURPRISE SIGNING:** Ademola Lookman **STAR STRIKER:** Timo Werner

MATCH ATTAX

PLAY TO WIN!

As every football manager knows, you need strategy as well as top players to be a winner. Here are five top tips to help you collect and play like a pro. You'll soon be a Match Attax master!

I'm a hat-trick hero!

1 **101 – THE ULTIMATE MATCH ATTAX CARD**

Look out for the 101-rated card in packets. The 101-er is unbeatable so it's a no-brainer to get one into your line-up!

100 Club

101   101

2

AWAY KITS AND HAT-TRICK HEROES!

Away Kit cards feature players in their team's alternative strip and are a must-have for your team. These cool cards could score you two goals meaning playing from home need never be a problem again. Also don't miss out on Hat-Trick Heroes, featuring players who've scored trebles throughout the season. They could score you three goals!

3 **SUPER SUBS!**

Each team has 11 players and 3 subs so if you want to switch things up, you'll need a good impact player coming off the bench. You can surprise an opponent and turn the game in your favour with a well-timed sub!

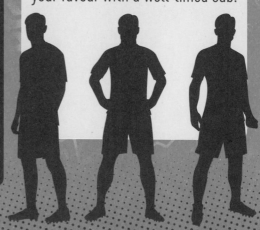

Let's go. it's time to up the game!

④ TALKING TACTICS

Change the game with Tactic cards. These super collectable game-changers include injury, referee and agent cards. They can damage an opponent's score, increase your transfer budget, make an opponent swap their player and even boost your cards. You're allowed to use two of them in each match so get them into your squad to take the win!

⑤ ATTACKING DEFENDERS, DEFENSIVE ATTACKERS!

Look out for players who are good in attack and defence, mainly all rounder midfielders and flying full-backs. These guys can spring a shock on an opponent out of nowhere!

MATCH ATTAX APP!

How to collect, swap and play with thousands of players around the world on the Match Attax App:

STEP 1. Search Match Attax on your App store.

STEP 2. Download the Match Attax App.

STEP 3. Scan codes found in Match Attax packets to get free digital cards.

STEP 4. Build your digital team and join the fun!

SWAP & PLAY TOUR

If you want to find out more about Match Attax, come along to one of our Swap & Play Tour events! You'll be able to swap cards to complete your collection, play games against other collectors and even take part in the Match Attax World Championships!

For more information about dates and events go to topps.com

ALL ABOUT

PARIS SAINT-GERMAIN

Paris Saint-Germain have plenty of heroes and pick up trophies every season. Find out why the French giants are totally fantastique!

TROPHY TALK

After four Ligue 1 titles in a row between 2013 and 2016, Paris Saint-Germain were beaten to the top spot by Monaco in 2017. But they charged back to their seventh championship in 2018, with Edinson Cavani, Kylian Mbappe and Neymar Jr cracking in goals left, right and centre! PSG has won all four domestic titles (Ligue 1, Coupe de France, Coupe de la Ligue and Trophée des Champions) and reached the quarter-finals of the UEFA Champions League.

PLAYER POWER

You'll see more stars in PSG's mega-expensive squad than if you look through a telescope at night! As well as their awesome attacking trio, Thiago Silva, Angel Di Maria and Julian Draxler boss Ligue 1 as their manager Thomas Thuchel drives them on in pursuit of more trophies.

STARS TO WATCH...

KYLIAN MBAPPÉ	**THIAGO SILVA**	**MARCO VERRATTI**	**JULIAN DRAXLER**
STRIKER	DEFENDER	MIDFIELDER	MIDFIELDER
Penalty-box predator	Cool head & top tackling	Ace playmaker	Skilful, with awesome energy

NEYMAR JR

His full name is **Neymar da Silva Santos Junior**.

Paris Saint-Germain's No.10 joined from Barcelona for a world-record **£200 million** in **2017**!

He hit the net on his debut for Brazil in **2010**, aged just **18**.

In his first **20** Ligue 1 games, Neymar struck **20** goals.

In **2011** he won the FIFA Puskas Award for a stunning solo goal for Santos against Flamengo.

In January **2018**, Neymar scored **four** goals in an **8–0** Ligue 1 thrashing of Dijon.

At Barcelona he won **eight** major trophies, including La Liga twice and the UEFA Champions League in **2015**.

In **83** Brazil appearances he has already smashed in **53** goals.

CAPTAIN: Thiago Silva **TOP SCORER:** Edinson Cavani (160+) **YOUNG STARS:** Colin Dagba and Tanguy Kouassi

PICK YOUR
DREAM TEAM

You've seen the most awesome and epic players on the planet. Now it's your turn to be the boss and pick your ultimate world footy Dream Team!

Germany international **Ter Stegen** has won La Liga and the UEFA Champions League with Barcelona.

GOALKEEPER

Your fantasy team will need a top stopper with mega reflexes and perfect kicking, catching and passing. Who will you go for?

Manuel Neuer, Bayern Munich ☐

Gianluigi Buffon, Juventus ☐

Keylor Navas, Paris Saint-Germain ☐

Jan Oblak, Atletico Madrid ☐

Marc-Andre ter Stegen, Barcelona ☐

Ederson, Manchester City ☐

Samir Handanovic, Inter Milan ☐

Alisson Becker, Liverpool ☐

Roman Burki, Borussia Dortmund ☐

Thibaut Courtois, Real Madrid ☐

Other: _____

TER STEGEN

DANI ALVES

RIGHT-BACK

This position needs an awesome athlete who can defend and attack and also has never-ending energy to cover the pitch!

Trent Alexander-Arnold, Liverpool ☐

Joshua Kimmich, Bayern Munich ☐

Dani Carvajal, Real Madrid ☐

Sergi Roberto, Barcelona ☐

Mattia De Sciglio, Juventus ☐

Djibril Sidibe, Everton (on loan) ☐

Kyle Walker, Man City ☐

Thomas Meunier, Paris Saint-Germain ☐

Elseid Hysaj, Napoli ☐

Joao Cancelo, Man City ☐

Other: _____

LEFT-BACK

A lethal left foot that can cross the ball, ping passes and make great tackles is top of your wish list! Time to take your pick...

Faouzi Ghoulam, Napoli ☐

Alex Sandro, Juventus ☐

Filipe Luis, Atletico Madrid ☐

David Alaba, Bayern Munich ☐

Jordi Alba, Barcelona ☐

Marcelo, Real Madrid ☐

Andrew Robertson, Liverpool FC ☐

Raphael Guerreiro, Borussia Dortmund ☐

Ricardo Rodriguez, PSV Eindhoven (on loan) ☐

Jonas Hector, Cologne ☐

Other: _____

KALIDOU KOULIBALY

Stick Super KK in your team!

CENTRE-BACK

Selecting two centre-backs from this list of quality defenders won't be easy! Which pair of players will make your dream team?

Dayot Upamecano, RB Leipzig ☐

Gerard Pique, Barcelona ☐

Diego Godin, Inter Milan ☐

Leonardo Bonucci, Juventus ☐

Thiago Silva, Paris Saint-Germain ☐

Sergio Ramos, Real Madrid ☐

Raphael Varane, Real Madrid ☐

Mats Hummels, Borussia Dortmund ☐

Kalidou Koulibaly, Napoli ☐

Virgil Van Dijk, Liverpool FC ☐

Giorgio Chiellini, Juventus ☐

Other: ☐

MIDFIELDER

Take your time to get the right balance from your three central midfielders. Speed, power, skills, and defending are the key things.

Harry Winks, Tottenham Hotspur ☐

Ivan Rakitic, Barcelona ☐

Luka Modric, Real Madrid ☐

Marco Asensio, Real Madrid ☐

Isco, Real Madrid ☐

Angel Di Maria, Paris Saint-Germain ☐

Mason Mount, Chelsea ☐

Donny van de Beek, Ajax ☐

Fabinho, Liverpool ☐

Bernardo Silva, Manchester City FC ☐

Arturo Vidal, Barcelona ☐

Other: ☐

Paulo **Dybala** scored against Tottenham Hotspur in **2018** to knock them out of the UEFA Champions League.

STRIKER

This is the most exciting thing about being a dream team boss – choosing the three fantastic forwards to lead your strike force!

Paulo Dybala, Juventus ☐

Neymar Jr, Paris Saint-Germain ☐

Erling Haaland, Borussia Dortmund ☐

Cristiano Ronaldo, Juventus ☐

Lionel Messi, Barcelona ☐

Luis Suarez, Barcelona ☐

Robert Lewandowski, Bayern Munich ☐

Antoine Griezmann, Barcelona ☐

Harry Kane, Tottenham Hotspur ☐

Tammy Abraham, Chelsea ☐

Mo Salah, Liverpool FC ☐

Other: _____

PAULO DYBALA

LINE UP
MY DREAM TEAM

You've selected your team, now is the time to line them up on the pitch. You can opt for some reserves and your dream-team manager too.

LB

GK

CB

CB

I'm a manager, not a teapot. What I say goes!

RB

SUBSTITUTES

MANAGER

LW

LM

CF

CM

RM

RW

75

BEST GOALS EVER!

Get ready for spectacular strikes by some of the biggest world stars of all time!

MIKAEL NILSSON

IFK GOTEBORG v PSV Eindhoven
March 17, 1993

- Incredible bending free-kick by the defender
- Nilsson smacked the ball with his right foot
- It sliced through the air and curled past the keeper

LIONEL MESSI

BARCELONA v Getafe
April 18, 2007

- The teenager took the ball in his own half
- Steered and slid past five players
- Drove the ball into the net

ZLATAN IBRAHIMOVIC

PARIS SAINT-GERMAIN v Bastia
October 19, 2013

- Captain Ibrahimovic showed great technique
- Crazy flicked backheel volley
- PSG cruise to 4-0 victory

RIVALDO

BARCELONA v Valencia
June 17, 2001

- Spectacular overhead kick in 89th minute
- Brazilian scores winner and hat-trick goal
- Secured Barca's spot in the UEFA Champions League

You can have this one for free!

Fantastic free-kick power!

MARIO MANDZUKIC
JUVENTUS v Real Madrid, 2017
Epic overhead volley.

MARCO VAN BASTEN
HOLLAND v Soviet Union, 1988
Sweet volley from a tight angle.

GEORGE WEAH
AC MILAN v Verona 1996
Rapid run from his own box.

JAY-JAY OKOCHA
EINTRACHT FRANKFURT v Karlsruher, 1993
Twisting and turning in the area.

CRISTIANO RONALDO
Rayo Vallecano v REAL MADRID
February 26, 2012
- Quick thinking by the Real legend
- Amazing backheel a long way from the goal
- Ronaldo fired Real to the 2012 title

Get me a tissue – I've dribbled everywhere!

ZINEDINE ZIDANE
Bayer Leverkusen v REAL MADRID
May 15, 2002
- Frenchman fired an epic long-range volley
  He helped Real win the Champions League final
- Incredible technique to strike the ball

DIEGO MARADONA
England v ARGENTINA
June 22, 1986
- Stunning solo strike in World Cup quarter-final
- The Napoli star dribbled from his own half
- Beat four challenges and shot past Peter Shilton

JOHAN CRUYFF
AJAX v Helmond Sport
December 5, 1982
- Cruyff tapped his penalty to the side
- Team-mate Olsen rushed into box
- Cruyff took cheeky return to score

LIONEL MESSI
BARCELONA v Real Sociedad
December 12, 2010
- Fantastic dribble and finish in 5-0 win
- Skipped by four players in the box
- Arrowed clever shot back across the goal

DENNIS BERGKAMP
HOLLAND v Argentina, 1998
Control and cool finish in the box.

ROBERTO CARLOS
BRAZIL v France, 1997
Swerving free-kick.

ESTEBAN CAMBIASSO
ARGENTINA v Serbia & Montenegro, 2006
Amazing team move and goal.

CARLOS ALBERTO
BRAZIL v Italy, 1970
Team move and crisp finish.

ANSWERS

P14 Path 4

P15

P18 1-30, 2-24, 3-23, 4-20, 5-7, 6-19, 8-38, 9-25, 10-27, 11-39, 12-26, 13-21, 14-35, 15-34, 16-36, 17-28, 18-37, 22-31, 29-32, 33-40

P21

P24 1) 3.45pm, 2) 19 minutes, 3) 3.41pm, 4) 4pm, 5) 56 minutes, 6) 58 minutes, 7) 14 minutes, 8) 88 Minutes, 9) 120 minutes, 10) 6

P25

P26-27 MATCH